NATURAL WORLD

CHIMPANZEE

HABITATS • LIFE CYCLES • FOOD CHAINS • THREATS

Martin Banks

WAYLAND

WWF

Produced in Association with WWF-UK

NATURAL WORLD

Chimpanzee • Elephant • Giant Panda • Great White Shark
Killer Whale • Lion • Polar Bear • Tiger

Produced for Wayland Publishers Limited by
Roger Coote Publishing
Gissing's Farm, Fressingfield
Suffolk IP21 5SH, UK

First published in 1999 by
Wayland Publishers Limited
61 Western Road, Hove
East Sussex BN3 1JD, England

© Copyright Wayland Publishers Ltd 1999

All Wayland books encourage children to read and help them improve their literacy.

✓ The contents page, page numbers, headings and index help locate specific pieces of information.

✓ The glossary reinforces alphabetic knowledge and extends vocabulary.

✓ The further information section suggests other books dealing with the same subject.

Find Wayland on the Internet at http://www.wayland.co.uk

Cover: A close-up of a chimpanzee.
Title page: An adult male chimpanzee yawning.
Contents page: A chimpanzee hooting in alarm.
Index page: A chimpanzee on the forest floor.

WWF is a registered charity no. 201707
WWF-UK, Panda House, Weyside Park
Godalming, Surrey GU7 1XR

British Library Cataloguing in Publication Data
Banks, Martin
  Chimpanzee: habitats, life cycles, food chains,
  threats. - (Natural world)
  1.Chimpanzees - Juvenile literature 2.Chimpanzees
  - Behaviour - Juvenile literature
  I.Title
  599.8'85

ISBN 0 7502 2454 1

Picture acknowledgements
Bruce Coleman Collection 1 (Gunter Ziesler), 8 (Rod Williams), 16 (Rod Williams), 17, 18, 21, 27 (Peter Davey), 28 (Gunter Ziesler), 32 (Werner Layer), 35 (Gunter Ziesler), 38 (Hans Reinhard), 39 (Christer Fredriksson), 44 top (Rod Williams), 44 bottom (Peter Davey), 45 bottom (Christer Fredriksson); Digital Vision 6, 31; Oxford Scientific Films 12 (Richard Smithers), 14-15 (Mike Birkhead), 15 (Clive Bromhall), 19 (Stan Osolinski), 22 (Clive Bromhall), 23 (Clive Bromhall), 24 (Stan Osolinski), 24-25 (Mike Birkhead), 33 (Clive Bromhall), 34 (Clive Bromhall), 36 (Stan Osolinski), 37 (Clive Bromhall), 43 (Mike Birkhead), 45 top (Mike Birkhead) 45 middle (Stan Osolinski), 48 Nick Gordon; Still Pictures 10 (Michel Gunther), 11 (Ed Reschke), 13 (Michel Gunther), 20 (J&A Visage), 29 (Michel Gunther), 40 (Michel Gunther), 41 (Michel Gunther), 42 (Paul Harrison), 44 middle (Michel Gunther); Stock Market 3 (Hugo van Lawick); Tony Stone Images *front cover* (Robert G Bishop); WWF 7 (David Lawson), 9 (David Lawson), 30 (Storm Stanley).
Artwork by Michael Posen.

Contents

Meet the Chimpanzee

The chimpanzee is one of the four species of great ape. Chimpanzees are found mainly in the forests of West, Central and East Africa. They live in large social groups called communities, each containing 20–100 chimps. Chimpanzees are excellent climbers, but they also travel on the ground.

Chimpanzees are highly intelligent. Of all the animals, they are the ones most like humans.

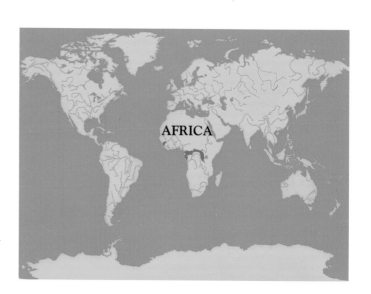

AFRICA

▲ The red shading on this map shows where chimpanzees live today.

CHIMPANZEE FACTS

The chimpanzee's Latin name is *Pan troglodytes* (pronounced 'trog-low-die-tees').

●

Male and female chimpanzees are similar in size. Adults stand about 1 metre tall. Males weigh around 43 kilograms, while females reach about 32 kilograms.

▶ An adult female chimpanzee and her young.

Arms
Chimpanzees' arms are longer than their legs. They are very strong, and a chimpanzee uses its arms to support its body when it is walking on the ground or climbing in the trees.

Ears
Chimpanzees' ears are very sensitive. They help to detect approaching danger.

Eyes
Chimpanzees have good eyesight. Their large, round eyes are forward-looking, like humans' eyes.

Lips
Loose, flexible lips allow chimpanzees to make a variety of facial expressions and sounds, which they use to communicate with each other.

Teeth
Chimpanzees have thirty-two teeth. They have broad molars for chewing fruit, green vegetables, and meat. Males have large canine teeth at the front of their jaws.

Coat
The chimpanzee has a coat of black or brownish hair. The face, palms of the hands and soles of the feet have no hair.

Body
Chimpanzees have broad and very muscular bodies.

Hands and feet
A chimpanzee's hands and feet are very similar in shape to ours. On the ground, chimpanzees walk on the knuckles of their hands and the flat soles of their feet.

The Great Apes

The chimpanzee's closest relatives are the other species of great ape – the gorilla, the bonobo and the orangutan – which are found in Africa and Southeast Asia.

Gorillas are the largest of the great apes. They live in the rain forests of Central and West Africa. In some areas, gorillas and chimpanzees are found in the same forests.

Bonobos are sometimes called pygmy chimpanzees. They live only in the forests of Zaire, Central Africa. Bonobos have thinner bodies than chimpanzees, and their heads are smaller. They also behave differently from chimpanzees.

◀ A fully grown male gorilla is known as a 'silverback' because of the silvery-grey hairs on his back.

▲ Male orangutans like this one are much larger than females.

Orangutans are shy forest dwellers. They live almost entirely in the trees and spend most of their time on their own. They are found only on the islands of Borneo and Sumatra in Southeast Asia.

Three sub-species of the chimpanzee are found in Africa. The only differences between them are the colour of their faces and the length of their hair. The chimpanzee is still the most numerous of the great apes, with about 100,000–200,000 living in the wild. This book will tell you about the life cycle of the chimpanzee.

A Chimpanzee is Born

▲ A young chimpanzee suckles milk from its mother's teats. It spends much of its time nestled against her chest.

After she has mated, a female chimpanzee is pregnant for between 200 and 260 days, about a month shorter than human pregnancy. She gives birth as she rests in a tree nest, usually at night but sometimes in the daytime. A female chimpanzee usually has just one baby, but on rare occasions she may have twins.

The baby chimpanzee weighs about 1.5 kilograms at birth and is completely helpless. The mother first bites through the umbilical cord and then gently examines her baby, carefully cleaning the newborn infant.

The baby is a source of great interest to the rest of the family, and they crowd round to inspect the new arrival. The mother holds her baby close, cupping it with her hand for support. She doesn't want the other chimpanzees to touch it.

Gradually, the baby becomes stronger. It is soon able to grasp the hair of its mother's coat, and clings tightly to her belly as she moves about. It also starts to suckle milk from her teats. The baby's eyes begin to focus and it takes an interest in its surroundings.

▼ A chimpanzee mother regularly inspects her new baby and carefully grooms its hair and skin to keep it clean.

First Steps

For the first three months, the baby chimp clings to its mother. By watching her face, it learns to copy her expressions of fear, anger and friendship.

Soon the baby leaves its mother for short periods and begins to take its first steps on its own. It never strays far, and its mother keeps a careful watch on it the whole time. She still carries it as she travels through the forest. At night, the baby sleeps cuddled in its mother's arms.

▲ Before it is six months old, the baby chimpanzee starts to ride on its mother's back. From there it gets a good view of everything going on around it.

When it is about four months old, the baby begins to try solid food, such as leaves and fruit. It reaches out to explore what its mother is eating, taking a piece for itself and chewing it to see what it tastes like. Gradually, the baby learns which foods the other chimpanzees eat. While it is learning, it continues to suckle from its mother.

CHIMPANZEE MOTHERS

A female chimpanzee may produce four or five young during her lifetime, giving birth every five to eight years. She continues to care for her previous children even after a new baby is born. Young chimpanzees often stay with their mothers until they have become adults, at the age of thirteen or fourteen.

◀ This baby is holding a twig. By handling and examining the objects around it, the young chimpanzee begins to learn about its surroundings.

Chimpanzee Families

The young chimpanzee is born into a family group called a sub-group, which is part of a larger community. The sub-group is usually made up of the baby's mother and her older children, other related females and their young, and some adult males.

▼ Female chimpanzees in a sub-group. They move around the forest together and help each other when they are threatened by other chimpanzees.

The closest relationships within the family group are between the mother and her grown-up daughters. If a single female with a baby has no female relatives with whom she can form a sub-group, she may seek the protection of an adult male instead.

As well as its mother, other chimpanzees in the sub-group also enjoy playing with the baby chimp. By handling and carrying a new infant, an older sister or other female relative can practise the skills of motherhood. But when danger threatens, the mother quickly takes her baby back again.

▲ The bond between a mother chimpanzee and her young is very strong, and lasts for many years.

Unknown Fathers

It is never certain which of the males in a group is the father of a new baby. A female chimpanzee will mate with several adult males – sometimes all of the males in the group – so her baby could be fathered by any of them.

▲ A mixed group of chimpanzees crosses a river. Adult males normally spend very little time with the females and young.

Even the father does not know whether a baby chimp is his own. He shows no interest in the new arrival and plays no part in raising the baby. This task is left to the mother. The father has little to do with the young chimpanzee until it is much older.

▶ If an adult male threatens a female or her baby, she reacts quickly to drive him away, screaming loudly and slapping at him.

Growing Up

By the time it is between two and three years old, a young chimpanzee is more independent. It can walk and run on all fours, and climb into the branches of trees. It can also recognize and collect food for itself.

When a chimpanzee is three or four, its mother tries to persuade it to stop drinking her milk. She hides her teat from the infant when it tries to suckle. At first, she gives in as soon as it cries, but gradually she becomes more determined. The young chimpanzee gets very upset, screaming and whimpering, and rolling about on the ground. But eventually it accepts this important change in its life. From now on it will eat only solid food.

▼ The young chimpanzee begins to taste different foods, but always under its mother's watchful eye.

► As the young chimpanzee begins to leave its mother for longer periods of time, it joins up with other youngsters of its own age to play.

Playing and Learning

Young chimpanzees are at their most playful when they are three or four years old. Play helps a young chimpanzee to learn how to interact with others of its own age, to become stronger, and to gain the skills it will need in later life. Adult chimpanzees are very tolerant, but the youngsters must learn to respect the adults. When they misbehave, young chimpanzees are sometimes punished by a light bite or a slap.

▲ These young chimpanzees have gathered to look at an avocado, which one of them has found. While they learn about their surroundings, they also learn how to get along with each other.

▼ These two chimpanzees are playing. The one on the right has a 'play face' – the chimpanzee version of smiling and laughing.

Chimpanzees spend a lot of time grooming each other's fur. This keeps them clean and helps to strengthen feelings of friendship and togetherness within the group. At first, a young chimpanzee is only groomed by its mother. Later, when it too knows how to groom, it begins to join in grooming sessions with others.

Learning to Communicate

A young chimpanzee also has to learn how to make the noises it will need to communicate with other members of the group. Chimpanzees use over a dozen different calls, and as the youngster travels with the group it learns when each call is used. For example, different calls are made when food is found or when danger threatens. Soon it will start to imitate what it hears.

Chimpanzees also use their faces to show their feelings. A wide-open mouth with the lips hidden is the chimpanzee's version of a smile. It is called a 'play face', and shows that it is friendly. An open mouth revealing the teeth and gums shows fear, while an angry chimpanzee keeps its lips pressed tightly together.

▲ This chimpanzee is showing the 'fear grin', which means it is nervous or upset. It may be screaming or whimpering at the same time.

▶ This young chimpanzee is pouting and hooting softly because it is becoming anxious. It may have lost sight of its mother in the branches.

TEACHING CHIMPANZEES

Because chimpanzees are so intelligent, scientists have tried to teach them to communicate with humans. Chimpanzees cannot talk like us, because their vocal chords are not like ours. But scientists believe they can be taught 'sign language', using symbols or computer graphics to represent words. Some chimpanzees seem to be able to make sentences in sign language.

Becoming an Adult

By the time a chimpanzee is between five and eight years old, its mother has had another baby. Even though the mother is busy looking after her new baby, she still maintains a close bond with her older offspring, through grooming and touching.

▼ A chimpanzee continues to live with its mother and her sub-group for several years after a new baby is born.

▲ The young female on the right is learning all the skills of mothering by watching its own mother with her new infant.

At eight years old, a youngster is about half the size and weight of an adult. It can fend for itself, and could even survive on its own if it had to. But the young chimpanzee will travel and feed with its mother for several more years. At night, it sleeps alone in its own nest.

A Chimpanzee's Day

◀ These chimpanzees are resting between feeding sessions.

At night, chimpanzee groups sleep in their nests high in the tropical forest trees. At dawn, as daylight returns, the chimpanzees begin to wake up. They sit up and look around, yawning and scratching.

The chimpanzees are hungry, and they soon go in search of food. Chimpanzees always know where to find the best feeding areas at any time of the year. To reach them, they may travel through the trees, or climb down to the forest floor.

After feeding for several hours, the group rests around midday. The adults relax by sleeping and grooming each other, while the youngsters have a chance to play.

Later, the chimpanzees move on again. After another long feeding session, they stop for the night. The chimpanzees climb high into the trees and begin building nests of leaves and branches. As darkness falls, they settle down to sleep. Chimpanzees build new nests almost every night.

▼ These chimpanzees are moving through the roots of mangrove trees in search of food. They keep in touch with each other by keeping an eye on their companions, or by using calls.

CHIMPANZEE FOOD CHAIN

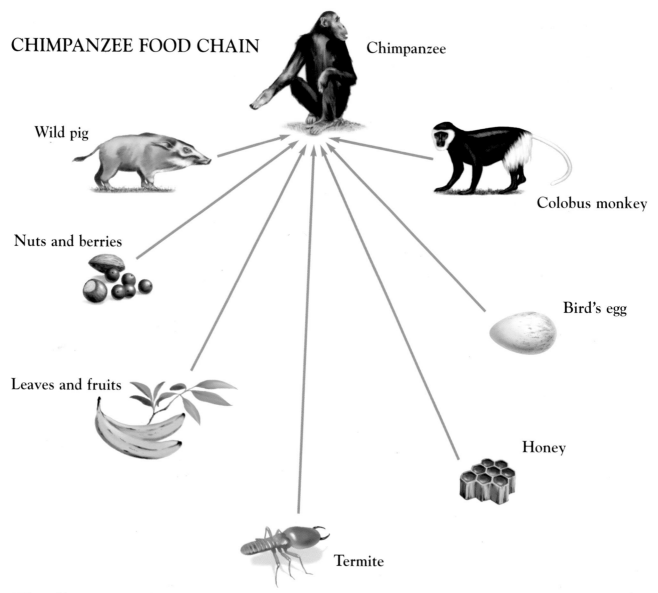

Chimpanzee

Wild pig

Colobus monkey

Nuts and berries

Bird's egg

Leaves and fruits

Honey

Termite

Finding Food

Chimpanzees spend six to eight hours each day searching for food. They eat a wide variety of food, but plants make up most of their diet. Chimpanzees feed on 200 different types of plant, and are particularly fond of leaves, fruit, nuts and berries. Plants aren't just used for food. A chimpanzee with stomach-ache will sometimes feed on a plant called *Aspilia*, which it knows will help to make it feel better.

▲ As well as plants, chimpanzees also eat insects, eggs, honey and animals, including monkeys, small antelopes, rodents and birds, which they hunt and kill.

Chimpanzees have learnt how to use tools to help them find food and drink. Some East African chimpanzees use sticks to hook termites out of their mounds, and wads of leaves to mop up rainwater that has collected in holes in trees.

▼ A chimpanzee using a stick to fish termites out from the trunk of a dead tree.

Chimpanzees in West Africa use stones as hammers to crack open hard-shelled nuts.

Rest and Sleep

Finding food can be hard, tiring work, so between feeding sessions, chimpanzees have rest periods. This is when they groom each other for long periods. A grooming session may last for an hour or more.

Young chimpanzees are very curious about their surroundings. During the rest period, they leave their mothers in order to wander and explore, and to watch what the other chimpanzees are doing.

▼ These two males are grooming each other. As well as keeping them clean, grooming helps the chimpanzees to feel closer to each other.

▲ A chimpanzee relaxes in its snug nest of springy branches and soft leaves.

Fresh nests are normally built each night, but they sometimes use them when they rest during the middle of the day. A young chimpanzee learns the skills of nest building by watching its mother as she bends leaves and branches to make a comfortable bed.

Friends and Enemies

Chimpanzees share the trees of the tropical forest with a variety of monkeys and birds. On the forest floor below live buffalo, elephants, okapi, duiker antelopes and other animals. Young chimpanzees and monkeys will sometimes play together if the rest of their groups are nearby and they feel safe.

IN THE SAVANNAH

In some areas, chimpanzees live not in the rain forest but in a mixture of trees and grassland called savannah. In this more open habitat, baboons often share their grassland territories with them.

▼ In forests and grasslands, chimpanzees often have elephants as neighbours.

▲ Leopards are perfectly at home in the trees, and are found in many places where chimpanzees live. They are among the main enemies of the chimpanzee.

A chimpanzee's main enemies are poisonous snakes and leopards. Even in the trees, chimpanzees are not safe from leopards, which are good climbers. However, chimpanzees' keen eyesight and good hearing give them advance warning of danger. When they see a leopard, the chimpanzees give loud alarm calls, and the group quickly gathers.

Together, the chimpanzees can usually drive the leopard away. Sometimes they hurl large sticks and heavy stones towards it. Adult male chimpanzees also have large canine teeth with which to defend themselves, and their jaws are as powerful as a leopard's.

Adult Life

Chimpanzees become mature at the age of about thirteen or fourteen. A female can then have her first baby, and the males can also mate.

Young adult males start to spend more and more time with the older adult males in their group. At first, they are treated as outsiders, but gradually they are accepted into male society. Adult males spend much of their time away from the females. They go on separate hunting expeditions and protect the group's territory.

▲ Fully grown male chimpanzees, like the one on the left of this picture, are bulky and heavy. An adult male chimpanzee is several times stronger than a man.

Each chimpanzee has its own rank, or position of importance, within the group. Adult males always rank above the females and young. One male is also usually dominant over his fellow males, but sometimes two or more will join forces together.

▼ This male shows off his long canine teeth, which he can use to defend himself if he is attacked.

How high up the order of rank a male rises depends on his personality. Often it is the most intelligent male, rather than the largest, who reaches the highest position.

Breeding

When she is ready to mate, a female chimpanzee develops a large pink swelling on her bottom. This is a signal to the males, who become very interested and follow her around the forest. The most dominant male usually mates with her first, but others wait their chance and several may mate with her in quick succession.

▼ This female chimpanzee's large, pink swelling shows that she is ready to mate with the males in her community.

▶ The dominant male chimpanzee is always the first to mate with a female.

RAIN DANCES AND JUNGLE DRUMS

Males often carry out wild dances to impress other chimpanzees, especially the males. They make their hair stand on end and stamp their feet, then they charge around breaking branches or throwing rocks.

●

Rain and wind often cause them to start this dance too. They all dance together, hooting and screaming as the rain beats down.

●

Chimpanzees also use the hollow trunks of giant rain forest trees as drums. They pound with their feet on the tree trunk and the noise carries far into the forest, telling other chimpanzees where they are.

Sometimes, a female goes off into the forest with a single male. The pair stay apart from other chimpanzees for several days. During this time, they mate frequently. This is known as a consortship, and it is the most likely time for a female chimpanzee to become pregnant.

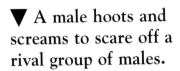

▼ A male hoots and screams to scare off a rival group of males.

Territories and Hunting

The adult males in a chimpanzee group guard the community's territory, which usually covers between 10 and 50 square kilometres. The males frequently patrol its borders, to keep other chimpanzees away. If they hear a group of rival males in the distance, they will approach quietly to check them out. If they think they outnumber the intruders, they start to hoot and scream to try to drive them away.

Sometimes, fighting breaks out among chimpanzees. Members of one community will attack or kill the members of another. Chimpanzees sometimes fight one another if their community becomes too overcrowded, and adult males may even kill infant males.

The males do more hunting than the females. Several males will work together to stalk monkeys in the trees. Some wait in ambush while others drive the monkeys towards them. The chimpanzees kill their prey by battering it against the ground or against objects, or by biting it in the neck.

A successful kill causes great excitement. Afterwards, the prize is shared between the hunters. Other chimpanzees gather round to beg for pieces of meat to eat.

▲ When chimpanzees fight, they bite, scratch and hit each other with their clenched hands and feet.

In old age, a chimpanzee spends more of its time sleeping and resting. Eventually, it becomes too weak to move about and feed.

Old Age

In the wild, chimpanzees can live for up to fifty years, but many chimpanzees die from injury and disease before they get old. A male is in his prime between the ages of twenty and thirty. Females continue to breed past forty. By this age, chimpanzees are often almost bald and very wrinkled, and the males in particular usually have very grey hair.

Old females usually keep their rank within the group, but males begin to move down the ranking system as they grow old. They are replaced by younger ones. Even so, old chimpanzees are still shown respect by their younger companions.

Eventually, an old chimpanzee becomes too weak to travel with its group. Then it remains in its nest, or on the ground. Sometimes a relative or close companion stays with it. Usually though, a chimpanzee dies quietly on its own in the forest.

▶ Very old chimpanzees often lose the hair on their head, especially the females. A white beard, and greying hair on the back and legs are other signs of old age.

Threats

The world population of chimpanzees is falling rapidly. Just fifty years ago there were several million chimpanzees left in the wild. Today, there are less than 200,000 left.

Chimpanzees are disappearing from many of the forests where they live in Africa because the trees are being cut down for timber. Some of these forests could be destroyed altogether within fifty or seventy years. Trees provide chimpanzees with food, shelter and pathways above the ground. As the trees are cut down and roads are built for the logging trucks, chimps are losing their habitat and becoming more exposed to poachers.

▶ Many chimpanzees are killed by poachers and sold in markets as bushmeat.

▼ Chimpanzees' habitat is being destroyed as forests in Africa are being cut down for timber.

BUSHMEAT TRADE

For centuries, people in rural areas of Africa and Asia have eaten 'bushmeat' – meat from wild animals. But today, the bushmeat trade is a major threat to chimpanzees. Poverty is forcing local people to kill more chimpanzees and other wild animals, which are taken to towns and cities for sale in markets and restaurants.

Many young chimpanzees are captured alive after their mother has been killed. These chimpanzee orphans are often smuggled abroad and sold as pets or supplied to laboratories for medical research.

Some pet chimpanzees die of disease and lack of nourishment because they are not looked after properly. Others are abandoned or even killed by their owners because they have grown too big or are too aggressive.

▲ These chimpanzee orphans, whose parents were killed by hunters, are waiting to be taken to a wildlife reserve.

The Chimpanzee's Future

It is now against the law in many countries to own a chimpanzee. When a captured chimpanzee is rescued from an unsuitable home it is placed in a sanctuary, where it can be cared for.

CHIMPANZEES AND HIV

In 1999, Scientists discovered that the HIV virus, which leads to the potentially fatal disease AIDS, originally came from chimpanzees.

The chimpanzees themselves are not affected by HIV, so studying chimpanzees may help scientists to develop a vaccine against the virus.

▼ Rescued chimps that have spent a long time in captivity will never be able to live a normal life back in the wild. They are taken to special wildlife reserves, such as this one in West Africa, where they can live in a semi-wild environment.

A number of African countries, such as Tanzania, Uganda, Ghana, Nigeria and the Ivory Coast, are protecting the rain forests by creating national parks and wildlife reserves. This means they can get more money from tourists, but it also means chimpanzees and other animals are protected, and timber companies are not allowed to cut down the trees. African governments are also trying to reduce the trade in bushmeat and stop the sale of illegally caught baby chimpanzees.

There are many organizations that try to help chimpanzees. Some of them are listed on page 47.

Chimpanzee Life Cycle

 1 A female chimpanzee gives birth to a single baby about eight and a half months after mating. The baby is carried by its mother and clings to her belly hair. It suckles her milk.

 2 Starting at the age of three to six months, the baby travels around on its mother's back. Here it can see its surroundings more easily.

 3 At the age of three or four, the young chimpanzee stops drinking milk and changes to a diet of solid food. It begins to live a more independent life, but still stays with its mother.

 **4** The young chimp reaches adolescence at about eight years old. It is still only partly grown and will stay with its group for several more years.

 **5** At thirteen, the chimpanzee is an adult. Some chimps now leave the groups they were born into. The females start to breed, while the young males may join groups of fully adult males.

 **6** Chimpanzees are in their prime between twenty and thirty years old. Males defend the territory, while females give birth to a new baby every five years or so. In the wild, chimpanzees can live for up to fifty years.

SCIENCE
- Adaptation
- Habitat
- Life cycles/families

ART
- Pattern and colour
- Group work – develop a rainforest frieze

ENGLISH
- Literacy – information retrieval skills
- Listening to stories about chimpanzees
- Letters to conservation groups expressing a point of view.

TECHNOLOGY
- Making musical instruments – drums
- Research using the Internet

Chimpanzee Topic Web

RE
- Caring for our world
- As a starting point for work on behaviour codes

MUSIC
- Listen to range of music from other cultures

DANCE/DRAMA
- Expressions and body language
- Mirror movements

MATHS
- Time – e.g. use information from the book to schedule a chimp's daily activities
- Use as a theme for mental maths problems

GEOGRAPHY
- Draw a map of the world and show the chimpanzee's habitat

Extension Activities

English
• Ask the children to collect and read a range of poems about monkeys and express preferences.

• Debate the issue of the bushmeat trade: one group could represent local people trying to make money; the other could represent tourists on a wildlife holiday.

Music
• Compose own music. Possible themes: rain forests and rain dances.

Maths
• Using the chimpanzee theme, ask the children to make up number problems for others to solve.

Science
• Introduction to a study of mammals and their characteristics.

Geography
• Find out about the rainforest habitat, who else lives there and environmental threats.

Glossary

Bushmeat The meat from wild animals.

Canine teeth The four long, pointed teeth at the front of a male chimpanzee's jaws, two at the top and two at the bottom.

Community A large number of animals that live together. In chimpanzees, communities are often divided into smaller groups called sub-groups.

Dominant A word to describe the lead animal in a group, which is more powerful than its companions.

Groom To clean. Chimpanzees groom by combing through each other's fur and picking out dirt, lice and pieces of dead skin, which they often eat.

Orphans Children or young animals whose parents are dead.

Prey An animal that is killed and eaten by another animal.

Rank The importance of a person or animal within a group. In chimpanzees, the highest-ranking male leads the group.

Sanctuary A safe place. Animal sanctuaries help injured or rescued animals to recover in safety.

Suckle A baby suckles when it drinks milk from its mother's teats.

Territory The area in which an animal, or group of animals lives, and which it defends against intruders and enemies.

Umbilical cord The cord through which a baby receives nourishment from its mother while it is still in her womb.

Vaccine A substance injected into the body to protect against disease.

Virus A tiny organism that invades the body and causes disease.

Further Information

Organizations to Contact

WWF-UK
Panda House, Weyside Park,
Godalming, Surrey GU7 1XR
Tel: 01483 426444
Web site: www.wwf-uk.org

The Jane Goodall Institute
15 Clarendon Park, Lymington,
Hants SO4X 8AX
Tel: 01590 671188
Web site: www.janegoodall.org

International Primate Protection
League, 116 Judd Street
London WC1H 9NS
Tel: 0207 833 0661
Web site: www.ippl.org

Web Sites

The Centre for Captive
Chimpanzee Care
www.save the chimps.org

Chimfunshi Wildlife Orphanage
www.infoweb.co.za./enviro/
chimfunshi/chimz.htm
A sanctuary for chimpanzees
and other wild animals rescued
in Zambia.

WWF Virtual Wildlife
www.panda.org/kids/
wildlife/

Books to Read

Atlas of Endangered Animals by
Steve Pollock (Belitha Press,
1994)

Atlas of Rain Forests by Anna
Lewington (Wayland, 1996)

In the Shadow of Man by Jane
Goodall (Collins, 1971)

Primates of the World by R & K
Preston-Mafham (Blandford,
1992)

Through a Window by Jane
Goodall (Weidenfeld &
Nicolson, 1990)

Index

All the numbers in **bold** refer to photographs or illustrations.